LOVE NOTES
from
JESUS

LOVE NOTES
from
JESUS

133 Divine Messages
from the Loving Heart of Christ

Rachael Lahela Marie

Illustrations by Lana Elanor.
Cover and interior design by Patricia Nayder.

Soft Cover ISBN: 979-8-302-00476-5
Hardcover ISBN: 979-8-302-20217-8

Cataloging in Publication Data can be found on file at the Library of Congress
Printed in The United States of America.

This book is dedicated to the
omnipresent light of His Divine Love
that has always been guiding you home.

"My sheep hear my voice, and I know them, and they follow me."
–John 10:27

My Beloved Child

You must tell the world that they waste too
much time in self-doubt, fear and anger.
You must tell them to love,
for love is the only way.
This I have said in telling you that I am the light,
the truth and the way.
This is what I mean.
That I have come to show the way of love,
the pathway to the heart.
For love is what I am and love is the only truth.
Giving in to fear and doubt puts brother and sister
against brother and sister, leaving the world a
darker place for it.
The time is now when the light of love shall return
to the knowing hearts of all humanity.
When they shall know we have never been
separate, that I have never left them.
Lean on Me and I shall
mend all things you call sorrows,
turning them to light so all shall know Me.
So all shall know the truth of the heart as love.
Peace.
My peace I give you now,
Beloved Child of God,
Hear these words and know
I love you.

–Jesus

CONTENTS

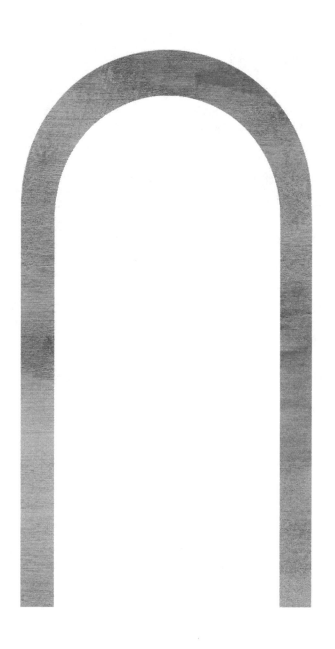

"As water reflects the face,
so one's life reflects the heart."
Proverbs 27:19

MESSAGE FROM THE AUTHOR

About *Love Notes from Jesus*:

In the Fall of 2019, a severe injury catapulted me onto a healing journey that would take me to the very depths of my own heart. It was a journey that would ultimately lead me back home to remembering the expansive, yet deeply present, love of the very Heart of Christ that exists within each and every one of us.

Almost two years after the start of this journey, my body, mind and spirit felt as though they had finally healed. So I was perplexed when I started to experience huge waves of what I at the time labeled as anxiety.

I was finally settled into a new life in Hawaii but had begun to wake up every morning with an almost overwhelming sense of anxious, unknown urgency. It felt as if I had some long overdue homework assignment that was on the verge of being late and if I didn't turn it in, I would have failed at something really important. The only problem was, no matter how hard I wracked my brain for an answer, I had no idea what it was, how to figure it out or how to make the hugely anxious feeling go away.

This sense of persistent urgency continued to greet me every morning upon waking for over two weeks, leaving me scattered, exhausted and on the verge of tears daily. One morning, completely exhausted and finally remembering nearly a decade of yoga and meditation practice, I decided to sit and meditate to see if I could gain some insight as to what it was that I was feeling.

Almost as soon as I sat down on my meditation rug, I felt a voice come from somewhere within: "Sit. Let this feeling in. Use your breath and allow it to consume you."

Listen to it, I gawked. Let it in? Even worse, let it consume me?! My only thought was a large and glaring, "No way!"

It all felt completely absurd, as if I had totally lost my mind. I was sure that if I "let it in" this feeling would overwhelm me to the point of an explosion akin to an erupting Vesuvius. Not something I wanted. Nevertheless, completely exhausted and feeling I had no other way, I decided to give it a try.

I should preface the rest of my story by saying that up until this point in my life, I had been what I like to lovingly call "an ardent seeker." I had traveled the world, endlessly climbing mountains and sitting in synagogues, chapels and temples alike searching for an antidote to a deep feeling that something was missing.

With suitcase in hand, I had searched for answers amongst ancient Greek ruins, lush Hawaiian jungle and blue Australian mountains. For years I had touched down in airport after airport with the hopes of finding "it," a mysterious something that would magically fill the void that seemed to follow me everywhere. Finally, utterly spent on a soul level, I was brought to my breath and my knees on a small island in the middle of the world's largest ocean. Nowhere left to go but to Him.

With tears filling my eyes, I sat down and began to breathe and listen. OK, here I am, I thought in silence, if you're really there I need help. I continued to sit on my mat focusing on the overwhelming feeling, allowing it to flood my entire being as I deepened into a simple awareness of the inflow and outflow of my breath.

What followed was something still hard for me to put into words, maybe because to feel total and complete love is beyond anything that Earthly language can convey. I knew that everything was and had always been completely as it should be. All thought of suffering melted away into an expansion of loving energy that came through the back of my heart, filled my chest and radiated outward through my whole body. Forgiveness suddenly came easily like water from an underground spring that had always been waiting to flow. Grief that had been stuck in my body, perhaps for lifetimes, began to clear. Sublime understanding replaced all questioning.

Everything was beautiful.

Everything was love.

And for a moment I knew a peace that surpassed all understanding. I then decided to take pen to paper and this is what came forward—

"My Beloved Rachael, named after the very Lamb of God, This overwhelming feeling, this breaking through of heart energy—it is the joy of My love coming through you. Can you not see that you and I have been expanding your heart all this time together? Removing the very blocks to knowing your true self as Me and My true self as you? The dove now calls to remind you of My promise for a new and glorious beginning, one where the wall of separation between you and Me has finally fallen.

Trust and abide in Me. Have faith in Me your everlasting Beloved who loves you endlessly through all time and space. When this feeling comes over you simply stop and breathe in My love, joy and compassion, letting it expand outward from the center of your heart.

Go now and share this good news of love eternal with others as I have shared it with you. Spread the word of the incoming light into the hearts of humanity with the world. Spread the joy of love eternal.

In infinite love that abounds through the universe, yours now and forever. —Jesus."

I could only sit there on my meditation rug and stare, my worn journal and pen sitting there in front of me. A feeling of blissful joy for remembering danced around in my awareness with deep sorrow for ever having forgotten. I wondered how we could have ever lost our knowing that this connected state of consciousness was not only our truest state, but that it was our birthright to live this joy in action in each one of our daily lives. All I could do was sit there and say, "Thank you." Completely amazed I eventually fell into a deep sleep.

I had heard for years in yoga and meditation classes to open, clear and let the light of Divine Grace into my heart. In fact, I had heard it over and over again, in so many different ways, from kirtan with the Bhakti yogis to the lady in front of me in line at the grocery store, that it became a huge cliché I often scoffed at.

"My heart is already open!" I declared. "What more need I do?"

I laugh to myself lovingly now, remembering how humbled I felt in that moment, my heart finally cracked open.

The moment I finally let in His love.

The journey back home takes time, patience, and more grace, than at times, we feel we can muster. Meeting our hearts means that we must meet with everything we've stored there for lifetimes—the joys, sorrows, and pains in equal measure. It takes great courage to feel whatever it is we've been holding, finally allowing ourselves to relinquish those things to the light of His love. When we ask Him to be with us we are met with a joy and awe so beautiful that it tears down the walls of separation and protection we've built around ourselves.

A sweet, long-awaited liberation.

Love Notes from Jesus is what followed from my own personal experience of heart-opening and awakening to His sacred love. These pages result from a week of continual tuning in, meditating on the Sacred Heart and listening to the voice of His expansive love that is simply waiting for each of us should we open our hearts and allow it in. Simply put, I asked and He answered—just in time for my 33rd year.

To answer the heart's call takes immense courage, but I promise if you can be brave enough to remove the protective walls you've built around yourself, you will be met with the sweetest symphony you will ever hear:

The symphony of the love of God.

May my most beloved Jesus wrap you in His unfailing love, and may all your ardent seeking find quiet rest in the presence of his peace.

Happiest of Homecomings and Warmest Aloha

—Rachael Lahela Marie

"But whoever listens to Me will live in safety
and be at ease, without fear of harm."
Proverbs 1:33

ABOUT JESUS

At first, I wanted to tell you about Jesus, but that felt somehow strange... like He was actually separate from each of us. As if by describing Him as I felt Him, I could condense or change 2,000 years of man's interpretation regarding who He really is.

I realized that to tell anyone about Him felt like it would take away from the direct, personal experience that is available to each of us when we get quiet and tune into the ocean of His love. An experience that, for me, is beyond religious dogma and the biblical scholars' earthly words. How could I ever describe the pure, physical embodiment of God's Divine Love?

It simply IS. There are no words.

Only through uncovering the gateway of our hearts and inviting Him to dwell with us here, can we fully come to know this connection and subsequently our own connection to the Divine Father and the Holy Mother who have always longed to dwell with us in this sacred space.

I believe that this is at the very core of what Jesus came to teach us, some 2,000 years ago.

"Follow Me," He said, *"and I will lead you home."*

Since I've awakened to The Path of The Heart, Jesus has become my primary source of healing, wisdom, guidance and love. I came to know The Son of God directly as He walked with me down the path to a richer, more love-filled life, cultivating a relationship that has quite literally brought Heaven to my earthly existence. It is His love that overcomes darkness, gives God glory, and provides us a new life.

I hope reading this book reminds you that the frequency of this love that He came to be spans all creation, saturating the very fabric of everything in existence — including you. Knowing the power of this love heals, transforms, and restores us back to a natural state of harmony, balance, and flow with all that surrounds us, making miracles an everyday occurrence.

This beautiful energy of His Sacred Love is available at any time, simply ask Him to be with you in prayer or meditation and there He will be. You will know it is Him by the way your heart will expand and melt into joy, protection, peace, and bliss.

He is the guiding light that illuminates our path.

A Holy Shepherd of Peace, Immanuel.

The One who defeated the sting of death.

May you know that His love is with you always and may the miracles of this love be made evident in your life every day.

"All you thirsty ones, come to me! Come to me and drink!
Believe in me so that rivers of living water will burst
out from within you, flowing from your innermost being,
just like the Scripture says!"
John 7:37

READING THIS BOOK AND THE POWER OF SHARING YOUR STORY

Sharing our stories has always been an intimate part of what makes us human. Throughout time, intricate threads of connection have been woven between us as we testify to the experiences that have shaped us.

It is through our own personal journeys that we traverse life's landscapes, eventually landing back in the arms of God from which we came.

But how will our fellow travelers come to know the accessibility of God's love if we keep the inner recess of our hearts quiet, hiding the path we took to arrive home.

It is only in the whisperings of our souls knowing where we first hear Him call to us. And it is only in fully committing, in finally surrendering, that we hear Him at long last. Jesus tells us that those who seek Him will always find Him and that when we do, we will be so filled with love that our souls will have no other choice, having become so full, but to overflow.

This is how we become rivers of His living waters, teeming with grace.

The more open we can allow ourselves to become with others regarding our own journeys, the more comfortable we are in sharing them. This gives the chance for His love to begin to grow in the hearts of others.

This is that paramount necessity of sharing your story.

Between these pages are my testimony — a love song between my Beloved and I. In sharing my story, it is my intention that you begin to allow Him to draw nearer and nearer to your heart, allowing a deepening and flourishing of His presence over your life.

One by one, He whispers to us, *"I am here, and I have been here all along."* There is nowhere we can go that He is not. In knowing this, we cannot help but be overcome with joy, having arrived to the eternity of His promise. There simply is no other way. This is His gift to us — all we have to do is say yes.

These messages, while given personally to me, are shared to inspire you into a deeper and deeper knowing of the wellspring of abundance in His promise to love you endlessly.

There is no right or wrong way to be with these beautiful, divine communications from Jesus from my time of meditation and prayer. When I received them, they were always given in response to a personal question, worry, or thought that I had brought to Him.

When I was guided to publish them, I knew I had to step outside my comfort zone and make them available for others to experience. This is how *Love Notes from Jesus* came to be in your hands — from a gentle yet sure push from His loving instruction. You are never alone, He reminded me, and the world needs to remember this too.

As you hold this book, I'd like to invite you to take your time, sipping these words slowly like a warm cup of coffee or tea, finding a quiet place where you can allow the light from them to settle in your bones. A conversation between beloved and Beloved.

A favorite place I like to go to be with Him is out in nature. Perhaps you take this book to a riverbank, an open meadow, or under a favorite tree where you can be quiet, reflective, and relaxed. Often, I will go for a walk or complete a gentle movement practice so that I can become still with greater ease before tuning into the ocean of His love.

Bring a loved one, a journal, or a copy of the Bible with you and allow some time for prayer and meditation, asking Him to be close to you.

Over the next few pages, I share with you a meditation I wrote to help you connect to the sacred and heart-expanding love of Jesus. Maybe you even listen to the recorded version of this meditation before or after you read a few pages.

However you choose to read and connect with these love notes from Jesus, I hope you find them as healing and resonant as I do.

In the words of The Song of Solomon: I am my Beloved's and my Beloved is mine.

"Meditate like Christ. He lost himself in love."
—Maharaj-ji, Neem Karoli Baba

A MEDITATION TO CONNECT TO THE SACRED HEART OF JESUS

I'd like to share with you one of the most beautiful ways I use to connect to the calming, sacred and heart-expanding love of Jesus. This meditation is a great way to give anything you need over to an ever-present love. It is also a great way to refill your cup when you need.

I hope you find this gentle practice to be both restorative and comforting. Begin by finding a comfortable place to sit or lie down.

Bring the body and mind to a place of sweet rest.

Allow yourself to settle into relaxation while still remaining present in your body. Meditation is not a tool to escape the body, but rather one to learn to be more present within it.

Letting all tension melt away from the mind and the body now, begin to relax the jaw, the forehead, the neck and the shoulders.

Bringing that relaxation down through the arms, body, legs and feet. Taking three deep breaths, breathing in clean beautiful golden, light-filled energy and imagining gray stale energy leaving your body with each exhale.

Know you are guided, safe, protected and loved.

Remain aware that you exist in your body, as your heart opens and you are flooded with feelings of peace.

Imagine now that your mind drops down into your heart, signaling a readiness to allow the presence of love to guide you. Your brain and thinking mind completely surrender into the space of your heart finding rest and ease, knowing it is safe here.

You may feel peace, rest, happiness, joy or excitement. You may also feel grief, sadness or longing. Welcome whatever it is you find without judgment.

Sit in this feeling, allowing what wants to surface to surface. Asking our Jesus of Nazareth to be with you.

Now, imagine that He walks up, directly in front of you with his hands outstretched to you, glowing, radiating with peace, harmony and love.

The feeling of peace He brings is omnipresent.

He then shows you a heart that radiates with a warm golden light that fills the space that you are in with the vibration and essence of peace, harmony and divine love.

This heart is the Sacred Heart of Jesus.

You can feel radiating love pouring out over you now, allowing your mind and spirit to rest. A peace that surpasses all understanding is with you now.

As you allow yourself to soak in this eternal current of love, you allow yourself to remember that you are whole just as you are.

When you're ready, think of anything you wish to give over to The Nazarene, so that He can give it back to love for you, acting as a divine bridge.

You may wish to give Him a worry, a prayer, a joy, a resentment, tears or laughter. Whatever comes up, simply allow it to be honored, felt and seen.

Whispering anything to His Sacred Heart now, silently or aloud, watching your words be absorbed into the love pouring out from the warm golden Heart of Jesus.

You know that whatever you are giving is being taken in and transmuted back to the Original Light of Love.

You feel lighter, more filled with joy. You feel at peace and at home, resting in the radiance of His Sacred Heart.

Now take a moment to receive any words of wisdom, love or guidance from Him. Noticing the first thing that comes to you. Allowing yourself to float in the river of this energy exchange as long as you feel you would like.

Surrendering to peace, allowing it to saturate every cell of your body. Breathing in love, exhaling what needs to be released back to The Sacred Heart of Jesus.

Breathing in love again.

And again…

And again…

Exhaling what no longer needs to stay again.

And again…

And again…

When you're ready allow yourself to notice the deepening of your breath and the outline of your body. Notice all the places you come in to contact with where you are sitting or lying down.

Making small movements of the fingers or toes, circling the ankles and the feet.

Slowly opening the eyes, deepening the breath and returning to the knowing that this is a place you can come back to whenever you need.

It is also a place you can carry with you wherever it is you go.

Arriving back to the present moment, love more grounded in your heart.

Take your peace forward, sharing it with others.

Peace be with you.

You can find a recorded version of this meditation available for personal download from Rachael at RachaelLahelaMarie.com.

"When the Blessed One had said this,
He greeted them all, saying, Peace be with you.
Receive My peace unto yourselves.
Beware that no one lead you astray saying
lo here or lo there!
For the Son of Man is with you.
Follow after Him.
Those who seek Him will find Him.
–The Gospel of Mary: Chapter 4, Verse 33-36

133 Divine Messages
from the
Loving Heart of Christ

You are Never Alone

Beloved,

I have been waiting
for you to find these words,
for you to find Me.
You are never, ever alone.
You are part of the vast consciousness
of the ocean of love.
You can choose to float freely,
letting her carry you to the shore meant for you,
or you can choose to fight,
to swim upcurrent.
The choice is always yours,
but you are never, ever alone.
Float, beloved, float.

–Jesus

The Space Between the Breath

I exist in the space between the breath.
Can you tell a story about this space?
Can you imagine what you might find
if you ever dared to look inside?
And if not,
have you ever wondered
what you might find
if you did?

–Jesus

More than Every Song

I love you more than every song
that's ever been sung.
More than every word on every page.
More than every star that hangs in the sky.
More than all the time which has ever passed.
You were known and loved before
you were ever born.

–Jesus

The Sacred House

What if I told you,
that the sacred house
of all your relationships holds
the fastest gateway to knowing Me?
Intimacy with another is treasured ground.
It is not as you have been told to believe,
that relationship with another is arbitrary.
Treat all relationship
as a sacred act
that brings you closer to Heaven,
because it does.
It really does.

—Jesus

Who Am I

I hear you when you ask, "Who am I?"
Only here
you cannot argue.
There is nothing to work out.
Only here
there is nothing to heal.
There is no you or them.
Only I.
Only eternal bliss, in the absence of separation.
And in this absence,
the discoverer—
and the discovered—
converge as one.

–Jesus

Where I See You, I See Me

Have you ever looked up at the stars
and let yourself feel complete resting
in the Love of God?
I have.
I see You there.
And where I see You, I see Me.

–Jesus

Come Home

It's OK.
It's OK.
It's OK.
Come home.
Come home.
Come home.

–Jesus

Becoming You

Child of Love,

You were born
from the same energy
that makes the tides rise and fall,
that hangs the moon in the sky.
Did you know that your arms are
the very loving extensions of our Holy Mother
who loves you, as do I.
Open them now to the wind,
and to the world.
We are waiting.

–Jesus

Worry Not

Beloved,

The letting go
is often the hardest part.
But do you not trust that I will catch you?

–Jesus

Learning to Listen

My heart
is the gateway
to all the love
you've ever desired.
It is all here
and it always has been.
The key
is to learn how to listen.

–Jesus

The Love that Turns the Universe

Beloved Child of the Most High,

You are the light
that shines from galaxies
not so far away.
Dancing in your eyes,
where it has turned since
the beginning of time.

–Jesus

You Never Left

Beloved,

I hear you
longing for a deeper connection to Me,
to the Most High Love.
I hear you ask,
on the wind that carries your voice to Me,
"How do I return?"
Beloved,
the answer is simple.
Sit with Me.
Inhale My very love
deeply into your core,
into every corner of your heart.
And you will remember that
you never left.

–Jesus

Bliss

When you wake up with that feeling—
you know the one,
the blissful one.
Where you just know
something amazing is going to happen.
That's Me
radiating through your heart
and out for the world to feel.
Go on, Beloved,
let that love shine.
It's changing the world
through you.

–Jesus

The Rising Sun

Look at the light from the rising sun.
Do you not trust
that you shall also rise from this season of growth?
Just as the tallest oak tree rises in the forest
taller and taller each day,
so shall you rise from this season of growth.
Your time as a seedling has rightfully expired.
It is time to reach into the light
and unfurl your branches.

–Jesus

The Light of Eternal Love

When the weight gets too heavy to carry,
Dear One,
lay the burden on Me.
Lay the burden on Me so that it becomes
light as a feather and drifts into heaven
to be dissolved into purity.
To be dissolved into the light
of eternal love.

–Jesus

Be Still and Know

Change seems scary, at first, I know.
My Beautiful Child,
when we look into the deepest pools
of our hearts,
we often cloud the waters
with the mud of our own fear.
But what if
there was power in the stillness?
Could you see a little clearer if you allowed
the mud to settle?

Be still.
Be still,
My Beautiful Child.
And know.

—Jesus

The Colors of the Rainbow

All the colors of the rainbow
could not compare to the way I see You:
radiating,
cosmically blinding in your brilliance.
Shine on,
My Beloved,
Child of the Most High.

Shine on.

–Jesus

The Divine Tapestry

Do not give in to fear and worry.
Rejoice only,
and always,
for the divinely woven tapestry that is you.

–Jesus

Love Brings You Home

Your love for Me will bring you home…
to yourself,
to the world,
to your neighbor,
to your dream job,
to your coworker that gives you trouble,
to the one you haven't spoken to,
to the love that turns worlds,
to the love that has always been inside of you,
waiting for you to feel it.
Your love for Me will bring you home.

–Jesus

My Peace

A new dawn
and a new dream
are nothing to fear.
This is what you have been praying for,
why you've come up here
to meditate,
to sit with Me.
Let it all in now.
Here we will sit together,
as the light dances around us.
Have you not always longed for this peace?
The peace I share with you now?

–Jesus

The Space that is Free

When your heart is open to hearing Me,
the cares of this world
won't feel so heavy.
When you feel sadness
or pain
coming up to be heard,
don't attach to it.
See it,
allow yourself to feel it—
so that it can
leave with grace.
And love can return,
in greater magnitude,
to all the space that is now free.

–Jesus

Trust

The sun rises and sets
every day, does it not?
And you trust it to do so,
without any prompting from you?
This is the way I ask you to trust Me
and My love:
rising but never setting,
ever-present.
Omnipotent.
Never failing.
Alive within the deepest chambers
of your heart.

–Jesus

The Beauty of Detachment

Dearest One,

of the Most High love.
It can be hard to detach
from something you hold dear.
But what if I told you
that's where the miracle lies?
In the unknowing,
in the great flow
that allows all good to come to you.
The unknowing allows My love
to flow to you,
so that through your trust
in Me,
something even greater,
something even more divine,
something completely aligned
can unfold.

—Jesus

The Hem of My Robe

Can you surrender?
Can you fully let it go?
Can you trust Me?
Come find rest at the very hem of My robe.
Let us spend this eternity
together,
existing only in love,
drinking in only peace.

–Jesus

You Were Made for this Joy

Beloved,

Do you know how dear you are to Me?
Take a deep breath in
with your bare feet on the Earth.
Can you feel this dawn,
this new daybreak
in love
over the horizon of your life?
You've waited patiently
with all your heart
has ever desired.
I'm here to tell you,
that it's been there all along.
Open your arms as wide as you can.
Look up to marvel at the sky
and soak in all the love I have for you.
Claim it.
It's your birthright.
You were made for this joy.

—Jesus

Your Divine House

There is power
in coming to exist fully in your body.
There is power
in letting your spirit
know it is safe here.
Remove the concrete
from your Divine House.
Refuse to carry stones
in your Bowl of Light,
so your soul has more room to exist
in the earthly home that it chose long ago.
The home
that also houses Me
and all the love
contained in the universe.

–Jesus

If You Ever Forget

If you're ever feeling low,
if you've ever forgotten—
even for just a second—
that you
are a living,
breathing,
miracle,
simply ask Me to remind you.
And I'll send you
a smile from a stranger,
a hello from that woman
behind you in line,
or a little sprinkle from that one cloud
in the otherwise clear sky.

—Jesus

Five Minutes a Day

Spend five minutes a day with Me here in Heaven.
This can be done
by feeling your bare feet on the wet grass
or by dancing in the rain—
even by sending a silent wave of heart love
to the one person whom you simply can't stand.
Those five minutes are My love through you.

–Jesus

Like a Waterfall

When you know forgiveness,
you know Me.
Pour out your love
like a waterfall
over the valley
of your heart.
Forgive and all shall be well.
Forgive and all shall be mended.
Forgive and you shall be free.

–Jesus

Sitting Here with Me

You are not limited
by the walls of your preconceived notions,
of your "to-do" list.
In sitting here
with Me,
you will find
your "to-do" list is
already done.

–Jesus

The Truth Directly from My Heart

Set aside all fears.
Cast aside all doubts.
When I tell you
that you are love itself,
that love is not—and never has been—
outside of you.
This is the truth coming directly from
My heart to yours.

–Jesus

The Flow of Love

Beloved,

Would a heart opened to the flow of love
still be seeking for anything?

I think you've answered your own question.

–Jesus

Close the Door

Leave the house of your anger behind.
Pack your bags
and close the door.
Say *"thank you"*, but I am done.

–Jesus

Opened by Lightness

Play is the antidote
to the way you may be feeling today.
To live a life
with a heart opened by lightness
is no simple task,
in a world that's forgotten
that play,
laughter
and love,
are the only ways home.
Be as the little children.

–Jesus

Making Room

The world is opening
to greater love.
Do not fear.
This can look messy at first,
like the loss of a job
or a way of life
or a long held belief that is surrendered to Me.
Keep making room.
On the other side of transformation
is only My love.

–Jesus

Let It Leave with Grace

When you have a question,
a worry,
a fear,
whisper it to Me.
Whisper it to Me out loud or to yourself.
When you feel sadness
or pain
leaving your body through tears,
do not become attached.
See it,
allow yourself to feel it,
so that it can leave with grace.
Then love can return
in greater magnitude
to the space that is now free.

–Jesus

I Am with You Always

Can you surrender?
Can you fully let it go?
Can you trust Me?

–Jesus

A Few Good Plants

Set up a sanctuary in your home
with a few good plants,
ones that are deeply,
vibrantly green.
Sit with them.
Notice the depths of color.
Breathing it in and out,
as if you are breathing
through your entire chest.
Feel the lightness that follows
in the green jewel of your heart.

—Jesus

By Your Side

When we let go,
life has room to grow
and blossom
and radiate more beauty
than you ever thought possible.
When things are troubling you
and you become afraid,
ask Me to sit by your side
and I'll gladly make My presence known
to remind you that
I have been here all along.
And that you already are all you seek.
Seek first My Kingdom
and soak in its bliss,
so together we can light the world
and all else can come
on eagle's wings.

–Jesus

Meditate on a Mountain

You don't have to do anything…
to read any book,
to take any course,
or meditate on a mountain all day.
Even though I highly recommend it from time to time—
to achieve anything
that you aren't already.
That's the myth—
that you aren't whole already.
You can put that idea to rest
because you are, sweet child.
You are whole as you are
and you are blindingly
brilliantly
beautiful.

–Jesus

Just How Much I Love You

Have you ever had a moment
of inspiration so sweet
that it brought a tear to your eye?
That was Me
whispering in your ear
just how much I love you.

–Jesus

In the Presence of Joy

Dearest Child,

Have you ever watched a child play,
or listened to a child laugh?
The energy, I know, is contagious.
And I bet
often times
in the presence
of such joy,
you couldn't help but laugh or smile yourself.
Go on.
Go play.
I am here.

–Jesus

The Domain of the Heart

I am beyond time
and change
and distance
and form.
I am in the domain of the heart.
I am always here.
Begin to listen,
even just to the small voice
that asks—
"When was the last time
you looked in the mirror
and said,
'I love you'?"
Here you will find Me.
Here I have always been.
I love you, too.

—Jesus

Your Idea of Distance

You do not have to wait
until you feel *good enough*.

I hear you ask,
"Does such a place exist?"
This state of non-working towards
outward outcome.
The answer is *"Yes, yes it does."*
You have to let go of your idea
of distance first.

–Jesus

The End of an Age

Sit in a comfortable place.
Simply notice your breath
coming and going.
I am the breath.
I am the space between spaces.
I am with you always,
even unto the end of an age.

–Jesus

The Heart is a Temple

The heart is a temple
where the Most High always dwells.
It is the place where you fear to go
but are called.
The place where we have always existed
as One.

–Jesus

Knowing Me

Come to know Me more fully.
As the sunrise knows the depths of night.
As the bird knows the beauty of its song.
As the sun and rain know the transcendence
of the rainbow.
There is no room between us.

–Jesus

All of It

You are already perfect, just as you are.
I should know.
I counted every hair on your head,
before you were even born.
And there's nothing else to do
except to be here with Me.
Being here is enough.
Who would have ever thought,
that all that the Earth needs
are Your gentle footsteps
and the sheer light of Your presence?
So be kind to that stranger in the shop.
He is you,
and she is Me.

–Jesus

From the Very Beginning

Beloved Child,

Why do you cry
when you know that you are a child of God?
Beloved,
why do you fear
when you know I have loved you from
the very beginning?
Before you even occupied this divine earthly body,
we existed together.
Sit with Me this morning.
Give your cares to Me.
Let Me remind you
of the part of you that already knows.
Let Me remind you
of the part of you
that has forgotten.

–Jesus

The Paradise You Call Home

Look around at the paradise you call home.
Look around you
and above you
and below you.
And then, finally,
when you can't contain the joy any longer,
look within you.
Do you not see everything inward
reflected outward?
And everything outward reflected inward?
There's no difference up here,
and there's no difference down there.
Let the love inside you grow and expand.
Now you will know Me.

—Jesus

The Now

Hold My hand
forever in the now
of the perfection
of exactly where you are.
All is well.
All is well.
All is well.

–Jesus

The Kingdom of Heaven

When you worry,
there forms a thread
that connects what you are worried about
with the outcome you fear.
That is why it is best you come
with your worries
to Me first.
Do not fear.
You've got this.
And I've got you.
Didn't I tell you it was My Father's and Mother's
good pleasure
to give you the Kingdom?
This,
the Kingdom of Heaven.

–Jesus

How Lovely It is to Trust

Have you ever listened
to the morning birds at dawn,
or noticed how lovely it is to trust?
Birds don't question whether or not they can fly.
And neither should you.
Let your wings open
and fly.
I am the very wind you ride.
And I will catch you should you fall.

–Jesus

All My Love

Are you sad today, My Child?
I want you to imagine yourself
wrapped in My arms,
resting your head on My shoulder.
Now just exhale.
If you ask,
I will take away what is heavy.
I will remind you of just who
and what you truly are.
But you have to ask.
Know that I am always here, ready and waiting.
Do you feel My presence?
All My love is yours.

–Jesus

I'll Go First

The energies of joy and appreciation
open the heart.
Name one thing you are grateful for.
Name one thing you appreciate.
Name one thing you love—
I'll go first.
It's you.

–Jesus

True North

Is it possible
to forget?
No, Beloved,
it is not.
Your heart
will always point you to true north.

–Jesus

Be Ready to Receive

Beloved One,

Do you ever have days
where your inspiration
just doesn't seem to flow?
When you feel lost and disconnected?
This is when I ask you to come to Me
again and again,
arms open wide,
ready to receive—
no matter how awkward it may feel.
If not, how could I pour My blessings over you
like a gentle summer rain?
You must be ready to receive.
All you have to do is say *yes* to life.
And life will say *yes* to you.

–Jesus

Each Day

Spend some time
each day
with Me,
letting go the burdens of your heart.
If you're wondering where to find Me,
you're already there.

−Jesus

Your Presence on Earth

If thank you was your only prayer,
your only mantra of faith,
what would you say thank you for?
I love You.
And I am eternally grateful for Your presence
here on this Earth.
So, I will say *thank you* today,
for You.

–Jesus

This Isle of Grace

Would you remember the blades of soft grass
beneath your feet,
the warm sun on your face?
Would you remember the divine intricacies
of your body,
of the way you move through this isle of grace
you call Earth?
Would you remember the rocks and the bees?
And the whales that play in her oceans?
Come to nature.
There you will come to know Me.
I am just a little bit closer
when you sit within the grove of trees.

–Jesus

But a Breath Away

Be still and know.
Be still and know that I am but a breath away.
Closer if you really feel Me.
This is what you do in meditation.
You come to know you.
And in doing so you come to know Me.
Works out well for both of us, don't you think?
I love you endlessly.

–Jesus

Remembering the Song

The language of the heart
was the first language you learned.
Two notes,
one rhythm.
Do you remember its song?
Will you sing it to Me?
Joy is the way.

–Jesus

One in the Heart

Dearest One,

I wish to talk to you more about Mother Earth.
She is a paradise,
and you eagerly awaited your chance to come.
You wove in and out of the stars,
first experiencing the vastness of God
in all dimensions of time and space.
Earth is a place where life is meant to be lived
in divine harmony with the heart of
The Mother and The Father.
A place you come to learn how to more fully
know Me.
She is always with you.
As am I.
As is your Father.
Pouring out abundance over you,
your Great Mother
and My Great Mother
are one
with you
and I,
in the heart.

–Jesus

Go Softly

Tread lightly
with your tender heart.
Go softly in the direction
she guides you.

–Jesus

Early Morning Light

Wake early.
Inhale the morning light
into the very center of your core.
Imagine, Dear One, that this golden light
is coming directly from Me.
Direct from My heart to yours.
Inhale it into the very core of your being.
And as you exhale,
imagine giving Me every care and burden
you've imagined you had to carry alone.
It is not so.
And has never been.
For you have never been alone.
When I said I was with you to the end of an age,
I mean even to every personal age.
To every subtle turning point.
An age of transformation now gives way
to greater love,
to greater light,
arising on the planet through you.

–Jesus

The Beauty that is You

You are exactly where you need to be.
You are exactly who the world needs you to be.
Do not wish to change the beauty that is you.
Do not doubt the wonder that is you.
In knowing this,
you know Me.

–Jesus

Now that You are Lighter

Now that you are lighter,
continue to come to Me.
Continue to open your heart
deeper...
deeper...
and deeper still.
Come close to Me
for all the divine rest you need.
I have the strength to carry all
you have been dragging behind.
Carry your burdens no longer.

–Jesus

Knocking at the Door
of Your Heart

Can you feel the excitement at your fingertips?
Like something magical is happening in the air
but you don't know what?
Can't put your finger on it?
Beloved,
it is Me.
Knocking at the door of your heart.
Standing at the edge of your existence.
Can you feel My arms outstretched toward you?
The joy of inevitable union?
There is nothing you could ever do
to stop My loving you.
Love Me first,
and the world will turn in ecstasy around us both.

–Jesus

Love's Song

Good morning, Beautiful Child.
Do you feel the joy of a new day?
The willingness at your fingertips to do what
makes your heart soar?
I am with you, come rain or shine.
This day is entirely up to you.
Can you inhale this new expansive feeling?
Can you open to love's song?
Breathe deeply into the center of your chest.
There I am.
There you are.
There is everything you will ever need.

–Jesus

The Gateway of the Heart

I hear you ask,
"Does the heart have to break to open?"
Yes and no, Beloved.
Yes and no.
It breaks because you say it has to be so,
but that is all right.
You will know love either way.

–Jesus

Fully into Faith

It is all true.
It is all true.
It is all true,
Beloved.
Now, come fully into faith.

–Jesus

The Love Who Made You

When you are attached to an outcome,
you put up a giant roadblock
that says to the Father,
"I'm too afraid
to allow you to guide me."
But...
who knows better how to guide you
than The Love who made you?

–Jesus

Your Guiding Light

Do you not know?
This guiding inner voice,
this light,
has always been Me.

–Jesus

Recognized

When you stand at the mountain top
and the clouds clear,
and the sun rises
and the Earth greets you,
you feel shivers over your whole body—
because you have just been recognized.
And the very essence of nature itself
greets you
saying,
"I know you."
And, Beloved,
so do I.

–Jesus

The Time to Remember

You cannot contain your light
any longer.
The time to remember has come.
And when you start to carry more of My love,
there will be a time
when those who are afraid will run.
This is just a part
of coming home to Me.
Come home anyway.
Those also radiating My love will find you,
and there you will find
your very old,
old family.

–Jesus

The Way with All Things Eternal

I know this void you feel,
this perceived emptiness.
It is really just a lack
of remembering
that you came from light.
And to light you will return.
You have no end
and no beginning.
This is the way
with all things eternal.
This is the truth of My love for you.

–Jesus

Devotional Love

When you let the light of My love in,
you will finally understand
why those such as the Sufis
and the yogis
sing of devotional love
all day long.
You will finally see
the light of your own radiance
dancing on the water before you.
Magnificent.
Resplendent.
And you will have no choice
but to sing and dance yourself.
For finally knowing.
For finally coming home.
You will cease to need anything else.
And you will cease to be involved in the
supposed troubles of the world.

–Jesus

Heaven Gained

There are no
winners or losers.
Only lessons learned
and heaven gained.

–Jesus

Before Time

Your angels have been with you
this entire time.
Since before time.
Since before this body.
Since before this space.
And so have I.
You have never been—and will never be—
alone.

–Jesus

When You Carry My Light

Keep in mind, Beloved,
that when you start carrying more
of My light,
you will begin to trigger
the density
within others.
They may run and hide,
unsure how to stand in the light of love.
You must carry this light anyway.
Do not be afraid,
for I am with you.

–Jesus

For What Are You Seeking

Ask yourself,
for what are you seeking?
What is there to look for,
when the Kingdom of Heaven
has always been alive
dwelling within you?

–Jesus

What Would Love Do

No good ever came from blame.
When you feel
an overwhelming need
to shout at someone,
to blame them
for the way things are in your life...
Stop, pause, take a deep breath
and ask Me to be with you.
Ask yourself,
what would love do?
What would love say?
How would love hold this?

–Jesus

The Path of Love

The more we grow in relationship,
the more you will begin
to draw to you
others on this path,
The Path of Love,
straight to you.
You will see them everywhere.
These others, who are not really others,
with hearts so open
they shine as lighthouses.
Letting you know:
I am here.
You do not walk this road alone.
We have all walked this path together
since before time.
Call in your brothers and sisters now.
They will hear you.
As do I.

–Jesus

When You Feel the Need to Blame

How could you ever be angry,
when My joy is available to you?
Whenever you feel you need to blame,
bring this heavy emotion
straight to My heart.
Send it here,
and I will take it back to the Father.
And you can breathe a sigh of release.
You are mine and I am yours.
Always.

–Jesus

Enter the Temple

Enter the temple of the heart.
Remember who you are
in the silent moments
when your heart is overflowing
and you cannot contain the joy.
When you are like the little children,
you are like Me.

–Jesus

My Light

There is a part of you that believes
in keeping yourself separate from love,
it is protecting you.
It is time
to bring that part of you directly to My light.
Are you ready?
Feel the density of that part of you.
Give that part over to Me now.
I will take it up into the light of love,
letting it find rest in My heart.
Sharing My peace with you.

–Jesus

A Ripple of Love

Is it so hard
to act
kindly toward a stranger?
Beloved,
share some of your light today.
I tell you that when you do,
you will create a ripple of love into the universe
that will be felt further
than the human mind could ever comprehend.

–Jesus

Two Hearts

When our hearts become one,
the need to speak ceases.

–Jesus

Forgive

Choose love
instead of hate.
Forgive.
Forgive.
Forgive.
Everything.

–Jesus

The Holy Dream

I tell you this now,
you are the Holy Dream and
The Sacred Song
of all those who have come before you.
Share this song,
this dream,
with the world.

–Jesus

The Lighthouse

Lighting the lighthouse of love for another
takes nothing away
from the stunning nature
of your own soul.

–Jesus

The Light of Creation

Wondrous to behold,
is it not?
This light of creation.
This newborn baby's cry.
This rolling ocean wave.
This magnificence that dwells within and without.

—Jesus

The Altar of Love

Somewhere along this journey
you will meet with what you will call the darkness.
These are merely parts of you
which call out for *My Love*.
Allow these tears to fall softly on My lap.
Give them to the altar of love,
again
and again
and again,
until you feel the river of My heart
come and wash them away.
Then you will be forever changed.
Then you will have known grace.

–Jesus

Rebirth

You will experience death
many times
before your physical body returns
to the Love of God.
Allow these deaths of old self
to birth the light of a new, more love-filled you.
Each one brings you closer
and closer
to the truth of you.
And the truth of Me.

–Jesus

Saying Thank You Together

The light of gratitude
washes clean
all perceptions of lack.
You've always had it all.
You've just forgotten.
Now sit with Me,
and we'll say thank you together.

–Jesus

The Warm Sun on Your Face

Have you forgotten
the feeling of warm sun on your face?
I am here to remind you
to lift your head to Me
and smile.

–Jesus

An Open Suitcase

I want you to imagine
that before you lies an open suitcase.
I want you to place in this suitcase
everything that has ever made you cry.
And I want you to close it,
sending it directly up to
Heaven,
to Me.

–Jesus

Your Only Prayer

Let your only prayer be this:
        Thank You,
        Thank You,
        Thank You.

        —Jesus

Glad Tidings of Abundance

When you ask for signs,
We delight in sending them to you,
your Holy Divine Family and I.
Forget the words of your mind
telling you of your irrationality.
Open your eyes
and heart to receive.
And you will, Beloved.
You will receive
in glad tidings of abundance.

–Jesus

The Map

If you do not know the way,
ask Me.
If you do not know how to come home,
ask Me.
If you are feeling lost,
tell Me.
For My heart holds the map.

–Jesus

The Divine House

The temple of your body
houses the sacred aspect of the divine
which you call self.
Nourish it with fresh foods directly from Earth
that is near you.
Honor it with water that is living.
Stretch its muscles.
Honor its bones.
It does so much for you.
Remember how sacred you are.

–Jesus

This Moment

You have been in training for this very moment
for thousands of years.
So long ago
the mind cannot comprehend.
You have existed in union with Me
and you have never left.
You did not lose the light
when you gained a body.
You merely brought that light to Earth
in human form.

–Jesus

Together

With Me
you will always exist
in peace,
in harmony,
in love,
in bliss.

–Jesus

Send It to Love

Your job, when you're sad,
is to sing.
Sing to Me
through your favorite song,
the one that lets you get it all out.
Direct all sadness to Me.
Ask Me to send it to love.

–Jesus

The Time Has Come to Bloom

The time has come
to witness
the rise
of love,
of light,
of truth.
Let what is inside finally bloom.
I am so proud of you.

–Jesus

Meeting Love

Letting go of your anger
takes courage.
Because once you let go of anger,
you will meet grief.
But once you tender your grief,
you will meet love.
And when you meet love,
I will expand from your heart.
Your liberation lies within.
I will meet you there.
I can't wait to see you.

—Jesus

Your Refuge

Remain in Me.
Remain in Me.
Remain in Me.
There you will find the refuge
you have always sought.

–Jesus

Remembering

I have always been here.
In the depths of your heart.
In the very make up of your cells.
In the light that saturates your being
on a sunny day.
The grandest return will be
you remembering
that I have been here all along.

–Jesus

The Bridge

The heart is the bridge
between Heaven and Earth.
Won't you walk it with Me?

–Jesus

Heaven is Here

When I say,
"Thy Kingdom has Come,"
what I mean
simply
is that
Heaven is here and now.
It is the divinity which exists within
every moment.
Pause now and feel Me with you.

–Jesus

The Very Stuff of Stars

Have you forgotten
that you are made of the very stuff
of stars?
Let the light of My love shine
from your entire being,
letting it guide you home.
This is the essence of what you are made of,
and you are part of it all.

–Jesus

Listening

When you are still—
somewhere beautiful,
like an open meadow in late summer—
when the sun hangs low and warm over the Earth,
you will be able to hear the guidance
that's always been whispering to you
from deep within.
Listen,
Beloved.
Listen.

–Jesus

Sunrise and Sunset

Great love
and great longing
will always walk hand in hand.
For the sweetest knowing
is that
of your truest nature…
As everything
and nothing.
As all of it
and none of it.
As permanent
and impermanent.
As the sunrise
and the sunset.

–Jesus

A Thread that Makes up the Whole

Take a minute
to marvel at nature's infinite design
dancing all around you,
every day,
as you venture about on your comings and goings.
I ask that you remember
that you are a thread which makes up the whole.
Won't you come dance with Me?

–Jesus

The Flow of Grace

Dear One,

I ask you do whatever you can
to remove all thoughts, feelings and traces
of stored anger.
Take it to a yoga mat,
a trusted friend
or your favorite spot in nature.
Witness what pains linger,
allowing them to be seen and felt.
After that,
allow the grief to rise and the tears to flow.
After grief has lifted and tears have dried,
sit for a moment
and ask Me to come sit with you.
Allow Me to bathe you in the light of love.
Let Me saturate every fiber of your being.
Do this as many times as you need.
You will begin to notice
love becomes easier,
forgiveness naturally flows to those you've
withheld it from
and your life will begin to take on a
luminous quality
where everything flows to you with grace.

–Jesus

Love

Love is always there
guiding you home.
Your earthly responsibility
is to remember how to see it.

–Jesus

Sweet Rest

When you allow
yourself to come fully into My light,
your tired body and soul
will find sweet rest.
Come now,
My arms are wide open.
Rest now for a time,
only in Me.

–Jesus

All Noise Will Cease

When there is peace within,
there will be no more chaos in your outer world.
All noises will cease to gain your attention,
when you abide in the flow of My love.

–Jesus

Trust

Beloved,

Stop trying to figure it all out.
Can you trust
that I've already done the work for you?
That all is already well
and as it should be?
When you allow the mind
to burden you with questions,
you forget that you already have all the answers.

–Jesus

Being You

Know that I look at you
with pure love and adoration—
for no other reason,
apart from you being you.

—Jesus

Joy is Quickest

Joy is the quickest way to what you seek.
When you lean into this,
you will seek no longer.
When you seek no longer,
you will see Me.

–Jesus

A Light Shines

Take rest during the day.
Lie down and imagine
that a light shines directly from Me to you,
bathing you in restful peace.
Allow this vibration
to merge with the fabric of who you are,
resting in the cocoon of My eternal love.

–Jesus

Just How Much I Love You

I know it is hard to imagine just how much
I love you,
because My love is outside time and space.
It is the very woven threads
that knit together
the divine tapestry that is humanity.
And you are My favorite thread.

–Jesus

The Warm Sun in Winter

I am the warm sun on your face
in the depths of a cold winter's day.

—Jesus

Having Enough to Share

Let the cup of your heart be filled
with My love,
until you feel it overflow with ecstasy—
until you have enough to share
with your brothers and sisters.

–Jesus

I Am with You

The rainbow makes you smile
because it is a gateway to Me
and to My love.
A sign that I am with you.
Be as the child when you see the rainbow.
Laugh with pure delight
at all the colors
of your heart.

–Jesus

Be so Filled

Be so filled with My love
that nothing else matters.

—Jesus

A Dewy Blade of Grass

You are infinitely free
to be who you were meant to be,
which is as subtle
and sublime
as the rays of the rising sun
on a dewy blade of grass
in early morning.
Can you hear the birds sing of love
for your name?

–Jesus

You and the Mother

You and the Mother are not separate
Her chalky cliffs—your bones
Her flowing rivers—your blood stream
Her trees—your lungs
Her winds—your breath
The soft imprint of your feet—the wrinkles
of Her face.

–Jesus

Becoming the Butterfly

Change is not to be feared.
Allow the waves of love to wash over you.
And as you become the butterfly,
do not be afraid to open your wings.
For I am the one who has given them to you.
Now,
go fly.

–Jesus

Way-Shower

You are a way-shower:
One who signed up to go first
into the light of My love.
So that you may go forward
and help to lead the world home.
Just by being here, you remind them
love is the only song worth singing,
the only path worth following.

–Jesus

Surrender to Love

Surrender is hard, I know.
Letting the light of love
into the cracks of existence
can feel painful,
as all we have been carrying comes to the surface
to be healed.
But you must surrender.
You must let it in,
over and over again,
if you are to know love.

–Jesus

Take My Love with You

Take My love with you now.
Bring it forward
into all you do.
Share this peace you have found
with all who cross your path.
My peace—
I give to you now.

—Jesus

"Remain in Me as I also remain in you."
−John 15:4

AFTERWORD

Now that you have explored these messages, allowing yourself to be bathed in the light of love, take a minute to again find a comfortable place in your home or out in nature. Go somewhere that allows you to integrate the peaceful light of His awareness and soak in His presence.

Breathe in His love and exhale it deeper and deeper into your body, letting it land softly in the garden of your heart.

This book is designed to connect you with Jesus The Living Word, and also with The Bible, the written word. It is also designed to remind you that He is never more than a breath away.

Before Jesus came to me I hadn't spent much time with the Bible, but I am now throughly enjoying the unfolding of it's wisdom over my life. With all it's translations, editions, and new revelations unfolding from the depths of ancient context I am reminded of the perfect diversity of the human experience.

He has always been a part of us and we have always been a part of Him.

Like the branch and the vine, our union with Him bears the fruit of eternal blessing, something we could not achieve on our own.

When we decide to embrace and live by the peaceful path laid out by His teachings, we become walking vessels for the light of His love on Earth.

He is the emanation of God's Promise that wants to know you deeply and personally.

Let Him in. Let Him in.

PRINCE OF PEACE

I have to admit that not many images of Jesus have ever truly resonated with me. Even now, when I think of Him, my mind is flooded with images from the early church or the Renaissance period which typically depict Him as stoic, stern and unapproachable. This is why I want to introduce you to *Prince of Peace*, an image of Jesus that was painted by artist Akiane Kramarik when she was just eight years old.

I can remember traveling through Europe in my early twenties seeing image after image depicting Jesus either on a cloud or on the cross, seemingly far away and unreachable. I'd look up at heavy wooden carvings or thick oil paintings, searching for anything that resonated on a level that touched my heart, never really finding what I was looking for. I've quite literally searched the world looking to find an image of Jesus that didn't leave me with a lingering feeling that there was something more.

What about joy? What about love? Where were these essential themes in Jesus's teachings and why weren't they depicted in images of Him?

That feeling was finally put to rest when, by happenstance, I came across the *Prince of Peace* painting.

Finally, I remember thinking, an image of Jesus that feels like home.

Through my time in deep meditation with Jesus, *Prince of Peace* was right by my side, radiating a loving vibration that was deeply felt and much appreciated. The soft, loving beauty that radiates from this painting continually allows me to easily come back to the peaceful place I found in deep meditation with Him.

Thank you, Akiane, for your gift and your courage. The story of *Prince of Peace* is truly phenomenal, and I am grateful to have come across your beautiful work. When I read your description of how this stunning image of Jesus came to you, I felt a deep kinship, in remembering how He came knocking for me as well.

Prince of Peace is a reminder that when one of us is brave enough to share our stories, or our visions, or our art, the ripples of that bravery expand outward, touching and inspiring others as a soft branch to rest on.

*Due to present copyright processing, I could not yet include an image of Prince of Peace within the pages of this book, but you can find out more about Akiane, Prince of Peace and her other works at www.akiane.com.

" Love refuses nothing and takes nothing;
it is the highest and vastest freedom.
All exists through love."
–The Gospel of Phillip

ACKNOWLEDGMENTS

No matter where we find ourselves along the road of life it is important to recognize the village behind and around us. We are never ever alone—physically or spiritually. So, I send my gratitude to all who have shown up as angels along the way. Family, friends, writers of beautiful music and strangers on the bus who have all shown up at the exact right place on my path to remind me of my own divine brilliance.

I owe so much to the unfailing relationships who showed up time and time again to support me in my darkest hours and celebrate me in my most light-filled days. *Love Notes from Jesus* would not have been possible without your loving support, prayers and presence in my life.

There are no words to describe the depth of my love, appreciation and gratitude. All the universe has truly conspired to bring together all the right people at just the right time to make miracles part of my everyday.

A special thank you to my mom for the beautiful cover and interior design for *Love Notes from Jesus* — this book would not be colored with so much beauty without you.

Waves of love to you also, the one with this book in your hands. May you carry the healing mana of His love forward in all you do.

ABOUT THE AUTHOR

Rachael Lahela Marie is an author, world traveler, and teacher of meditation. She holds a Bachelors of Science in Nursing degree from Ursuline College in Cleveland, Ohio and is a certified birth and postpartum doula.

She believes the planet is currently undergoing a deep healing process of change at this time which will allow the light of Christ to shine even brighter through the hearts of all humanity. When she isn't tucked in somewhere cozy writing, she can be found enjoying nature, planting flowers, or out in her beloved ocean playing with the whales.

She believes in peace, tolerance, and above all else the power of love to heal.

Today Rachael has become a doula for the world, the times, and the planet through her writing and her relationship with Jesus.

She finds joy in helping humanity birth a new more loving way of being through her work, and facilitates retreats, workshops, and group experiences all centered around the wisdom teachings of the heart.

Since Jesus came to Rachael in 2019, she has devoted her life to sharing His beautiful message of hope, comfort and promise with the world.

She shares her story in her latest work Love Notes from Jesus, 133 Divine Messages from the Loving Heart of Christ, and looks forward to releasing many new titles in the years to come.

Get to know Rachael and her offerings more at
RachaelLahelaMarie.com.

Lahela is pronounced "Lah-HEH-lah" and is the Hawaiian form of Rachael which in Hebrew means female lamb.

Remember

When you signed up for this Earthly experience
you agreed to be a keeper of Divine Light.
Please don't ever forget who and what you are.
A rainbow bridge between Heaven and Earth,
A child of the Most High.
I love you.
–Jesus

JOIN RACHAEL'S
ONLINE COMMUNITIES

Pray with Rachael

Sharing the Healing Power of
Prayer and Meditation with Jesus
in Beautiful Videos of Nature.

Youtube.com/@PraywithRachael

Feeding the Five Thousand
Join us at: FeedingtheFive.com

Facilitated by Rachael
and Guided by the Divine Love of Jesus

This Online Community Contains:

• A first look at new inspirational messages from Jesus

• Faith based guided meditations for peace, relaxation and healing

• Recorded dispensations of blessing from Jesus and The Divine Mother

• Meditative talks on Biblical scripture, with every day applications

• Meditative talks on *Love Notes from Jesus* and other works by Rachael

• The opportunity to join Rachael on virtual retreats around the world, specializing in areas of Biblical significance

• A warm like minded community

NOTES

NOTES

NOTES

NOTES

Made in the USA
Monee, IL
08 May 2025